Table of Content

Introduction

Welcome to "How to Make Passive Income with Zero Money"! This e-book will explore various ways to generate passive income streams without investing a lot of money upfront.

But before diving into the specifics, let's define passive income. Passive income is money earned without the need for continual labour or maintenance. Money continues to flow in even when you are not actively working. That can take the shape of interest, dividends, or rental income, among other things.

There are many benefits to generating passive income. It can provide financial security and freedom. It may bring financial stability and independence and allow you to diversify your revenue sources and dedicate more time to other pursuits.

Unfortunately, many believe it takes a lot of money to generate passive income. That is not true. There are numerous ways to make passive income with zero money upfront, and we will explore them in this e-book. So, if you're ready to learn how to start building your passive income streams,

let's get started!

Chapter 1: The Benefits of Passive Income Streams

The term "passive income" refers to any source of earnings that doesn't necessitate constant, active work on your part. Passive income is an alternative to regular employment in which your time and effort are directly proportional to your hourly compensation or salary. Improve one's financial security and independence; this might offer several advantages.

The capacity to earn revenue regularly is a significant perk of passive income streams. A person's passive income stream may be more consistent than their active revenue stream, which may fluctuate depending on factors such as the number of hours worked, or the number of clients served. Particularly helpful for people aiming to augment their active income or gain economic independence.

In addition to helping, you save time and effort, passive income streams provide you with more freedom and control over your professional and personal life. The main difference between active and passive income is that the latter does not require you to be physically present to generate funds. That might give you more time to focus on hobbies, travel, or do whatever makes you happy.

Passive income sources not only provide a reliable and malleable source of funding but also have the potential to generate substantial sums. The work involved in establishing many sources of passive income can be worthwhile in the long term. Real estate rentals, dividend-paying equities, and internet enterprises are a few passive income streams that have enabled many successful entrepreneurs and investors to amass substantial wealth.

Passive income streams may be invaluable for bolstering one's financial security and independence. You may develop a steady stream of income that requires no maintenance by accumulating various passive income streams.

Chapter 2: Ideas for Generating Passive Income with Zero Money Upfront

While it may appear challenging to get passive income with no initial commitment, various options are available.

Consider the following suggestions:

Sell items or services on a platform that charges a commission:

Many internet platforms allow you to offer items or services for free. You can, for example, open an Etsy or eBay account and sell handmade or vintage products. On platforms like Fiverr or Upwork, you may also provide writing, graphic design, or photography skills. While some networks take a share of the transaction, you may start earning money now.

Create a blog or a YouTube channel:

If you are enthusiastic about a specific topic or pastime, you can create a blog or a YouTube channel and earn passive money through advertising and sponsored content. While acquiring a following may take some time, this may be a terrific method to monetize your hobbies and expertise with no out-of-pocket expenses.

Utilize social media to sell products or services:

If you have a significant social media following, you can use your platform to sell products or services and earn a percentage of sales. You may join an affiliate for a specific business and make a portion of the sale by promoting their items on your social media.

Airbnb a room:

If you have a spare room, you may generate passive money by renting it out on Airbnb. Because Airbnb handles the booking and payment processes, this might be a terrific method to make money with no upfront fees.

While some initial effort is required to get these ideas off the ground, they may give a terrific opportunity to produce passive income with no money out of pocket. You may build a dependable source of income by utilizing your talents and hobbies with no upfront commitment.

Chapter 3: Case studies of Individuals who have Successfully Developed Passive Income with Little to no upfront Investment

Creating passive income streams can be an excellent method to earn money without actively exchanging your time for money. Setting up passive income streams may require some initial work, but the long-term advantages are well worth it. This article will look at five case studies of people who have effectively created passive income with little to no initial commitment.

Case Study #1:

Sarah, the Blogger, is the first case study. Sarah had always liked writing, but she had never considered it as a source of passive income. Sarah created a blog about her trips and adventures one day. She launched her blog using free platforms such as WordPress and Blogger and began sharing her experiences and ideas.

Sarah earned money through advertising and sponsored content as her site rose in popularity. She also wrote an e-book and an online course, which she marketed on her blog and other areas such as Udemy and Teachable. Sarah eventually transformed her passion into a passive income stream that brought her hundreds of dollars monthly.

Case Study #2:

Podcaster Jack-Jack had always been fascinated by music and loved discussing it with his pals. He decided to establish a podcast on his favourite bands and artists and recorded and edited his episodes using free tools such as Audacity.

Jack's podcast grew in popularity, so he made money through sponsorships and advertising. He has established a premium subscription service, which provides listeners with unique material and goods. Each month, Jack's podcast earns thousands of dollars in passive revenue.

Case Study #3:

Rachel, the E-book Author. Rachel was an ardent reader who loved writing short tales and essays in her spare time. She combined her interests and published an e-book on her college experiences.

Rachel created her e-book with free tools like Google Docs and Canva and released it on sites like Amazon Kindle Direct Publishing and Apple Books. She also advertised her e-book on social media and in online writing forums. Because of her e-book sales, Rachel was able to establish a consistent source of passive income.

Case Study #4:

David, the YouTube Creator David, had always been interested in video production and editing, and he liked sharing his work with his friends. He created a YouTube account to share his videos with a larger audience.

David began his YouTube career by creating and editing movies with free tools such as iMovie and Adobe Premiere. As his channel's popularity rose, he began earning money through advertising and sponsorships. He also set up a Patreon website, where his most devoted followers could support him with monthly payments. David's YouTube channel now earns several thousand dollars monthly in passive revenue.

Case Study #5:

Emily, the App Developer. Emily has always been interested in technology and has liked coding issues. She used her abilities by developing simple software that allowed individuals to track their regular water intake.

Emily created her software with free tools like Xcode and Android Studio and launched it on the App Store and Google Play. She also advertised her software on social media and in internet forums. Due to her software sales and in-app purchases, Emily could produce a consistent source of passive income.

Finally, these five case studies show that creating passive income streams with little to no initial commitment is feasible. Whether you like writing, podcasting, video creation, or software development, you may convert your hobbies into a source of passive income. You, too, can create a passive income stream that delivers financial freedom and security with dedication and hard work.

Chapter 4: Selling Physical Products on a Third-Party Platform

If you have a knack for creating or finding unique and exciting products, then selling physical items on a third-party platform could be a great way to make passive income with zero money upfront.

Here are some examples of popular platforms where you can sell physical products:

- Etsy: Etsy is an e-commerce platform for unique and vintage things. Craft supplies are also available. It's an excellent place for artists, artisans, and small business owners to market their handcrafted or one-of-a-kind items.

- eBay: eBay is a global online marketplace where you can sell just about anything. It is a good option if you have a large inventory of products or want to sell products in high demand.

- Amazon: Amazon is the world's largest online retailer and offers various ways to sell physical products. You can sell your products through the Amazon Marketplace or use the Amazon Handmade or Amazon FBA (Fulfillment by Amazon) programs to sell handmade or unique items.

Now that you have an idea of some of the platforms available, here are some tips for success when selling physical products on a third-party platform:

- Research demand: Before you start selling, make sure there is a market for the products you want to sell. Examine what is already available for sale on the platform to see if you can fill a market need.

- Price your products correctly: Determine the cost of your products and add a reasonable profit margin. Remember that your prices should be competitive with similar products on the platform.

- Market your products: Once you have them listed, promote them to potential customers. Utilize the platform's built-in marketing tools and consider using social media or other marketing channels to reach a wider audience.

Chapter 5: Selling Digital Products on a Third-Party Platform

Selling digital products is another great way to make passive income with zero upfront money. Digital products are easy to create and can be sold repeatedly without additional costs. Here are some examples of platforms where you can sell digital products:

- **Etsy**: Etsy is not just a marketplace for physical products. It also allows you to sell digital products such as printables, templates, and design elements.

- **eBay**: eBay allows you to sell digital products such as ebooks, music, and software.

- **Creative Market**: Creative Market is an online store for digital design tools such as fonts, images, and templates.

Now that you have an idea of some of the platforms available, here are some tips for success when selling digital products on a third-party platform:

- **Research demand:** As with physical products, it is crucial to ensure that there is a market for the digital products you want to sell. Study what is currently traded on the network to discover if there is a market gap that you may fill.
- **Price your products correctly:** Determine the value of your products and set your prices accordingly. Remember that your costs should be competitive with similar products on the platform.

- **Market your products:** Once you have them listed, promote them to potential customers. Utilize the platform's built-in marketing tools and consider using social media or other marketing channels to reach a wider audience.

Remember that creating high-quality, value items that solve a problem or satisfy your client's needs is the key to success when selling digital products.

Chapter 6: Selling Products or Services on Your Website

Suppose you want more control over your online store and the customer experience. In that case, setting up an e-commerce website might be the right option. To get started, consider the following steps:

1. Choose an e-commerce platform: Many options are available, such as Shopify, WooCommerce, and Magento. Analyze and compare the features and cost of each forum to pick the one that best meets your requirements. These trying to follow are

some things to think about while choosing a venue:

- **Ease of use**: Look for a user-friendly and easy-to-navigate platform, especially if you are new to e-commerce

- **Integration with payment gateways**: Make sure your chosen platform is compatible with the payment gateways you want to use, such as PayPal or Stripe.

- **Features**: Consider the features each platform offers, such as inventory management, shipping options, and customer reviews.

2. Set up your website: Follow the platform's instructions for setting up your website, including choosing a domain name, selecting a theme, and adding your products. Make sure to include clear product descriptions, high-quality images, and pricing information. Consider hiring a professional to design your website if you need more confidence in your design skills.

3. Choose a payment gateway: Choose a payment gateway suitable for your e-

commerce platform that can accept various payment methods, including credit cards and PayPal. Research and compare the fees and features of different payment gateways to find the one that best fits your needs.

4. Market your website: Once your website is complete and your products are listed, it's time to start promoting your store to potential customers. Use social media and other marketing tools to reach a larger audience and generate traffic to your website.

Here are some tips for success when selling products or services on your website:

- Choose a niche: It is critical to specialize in a particular sector or type of product to differentiate from the competitive market and develop a loyal client base. Consider what you are passionate about or your expertise and build your store around that.

- Build an audience: Consider offering free resources or running promotions to attract potential customers and build your email list. You can then use this list to promote your products and inform your customers about new offerings.

- Market your products: To attract a larger audience and boost traffic to your website, use various marketing methods such as social media, email marketing, and paid advertising. Feel free to experiment with marketing strategies to see what works best for your business.

Remember that building a successful e-commerce business takes time and effort. Maintain your patience and focus on your goals. You'll then be well on the way to generating passive income from your online business.

Chapter 7: Self-publishing a book on Amazon

Self-publishing an e-book on Amazon is a great way to get your work out into the world and make it available to a broad audience of readers.

Amazon's Kindle Direct Publishing (KDP) platform makes it easy to upload your e-book and start selling it to readers worldwide. In this section, we'll provide an overview of the process for creating and publishing an e-book on KDP.

First, let's start with how to create a KDP account. To get started, visit the KDP website and top right, click the "Sign In" button right corner you do not have an Amazon account, create one. You'll need to create one by entering your email address and creating a password. Once you have an Amazon account, you can use it to sign in to KDP and start the process of self-publishing your e-book.

Before uploading your e-book to KDP, you'll need to create the e-book file. You can use a few file formats for your e-book, including .doc, .pdf, and .epub. The most generally recognized and recommended form for most e-books is .epub. You can use a tool like Microsoft Word or Adobe InDesign to create your e-book file or hire a designer to do it for you.

Once your e-book file is ready, you can upload it to KDP using the "Add New Title" button. You'll be requested to provide basic information about your e-books, such as the title, author name, and description. You'll also need to choose a category for your e-book, which will help it appear in relevant search results.

One of the great things about KDP is that it allows you to set the price of your e-book and choose from a range of royalty options. You can set the price at any amount you like, but keep in mind that lower prices may lead to more sales. Depending on how much your e-book costs and where you buy it, you could receive a royalty rate of 35% or 70%.

Aside from creating and submitting your e-book, you can do a few more things to improve your chances of success on KDP. Writing a compelling e-book is crucial, as it will help grab readers' attention and keep them engaged. When submitting your e-book to KDP, selecting the appropriate category, and utilizing relevant keywords is also a good idea. That will help ensure that it appears in relevant search results and is more likely to be discovered by potential readers.

Marketing is also essential when self-publishing an e-book on Amazon. You can promote your e-book through social media, email marketing, and running ads on platforms like Facebook and Google. You can also reach out to bloggers and book review websites to see if they would be interested in reviewing your e-book.

In conclusion, self-publishing an e-book on Amazon is a great way to get your work out into the world and make it available to a broad audience of readers. Following the tips in this section can increase your chances of success and reach a larger audience with your e-book.

Chapter 8: Creating and selling an online course or workshop

Creating and selling an online course or workshop can be a great way to share your expertise with a broader audience and generate passive income. Several platforms allow you to create and sell online courses, including Udemy, Skillshare, and Teachable. This section will provide an overview of these platforms and offer some tips for success when creating and selling an online course or workshop.

First, look at some of the most popular platforms for creating and selling online courses. Udemy is a well-known platform that allows anyone to create and sell online courses on various topics. Skillshare is like Udemy but focuses on creative and design-related methods. Teachable is another popular platform that offers a range of tools and features for creating and selling online courses.

Now, let's talk about how to make an online course or workshop. The first step is to select an in-demand topic you know. Before you begin producing your class or workshop, you must research to ensure that there is a demand for it.

Once you have chosen a topic, the next step is to create your course or workshop content. That can include videos, slides, audio recordings, and any other materials you want to have. It's essential to make your content engaging and interactive, as this will help keep your students interested and motivated.

Once you have created your course or workshop content, you can upload it to one of the platforms we mentioned earlier, such as Udemy, Skillshare, or Teachable. Each platform has its process for uploading courses, but they generally involve creating an account, filling out some basic information about your module, and uploading your content.

Finally, let's talk about some tips for success when creating and selling an online course or workshop. Choosing a popular topic is one of the most crucial things you can do. That means researching and discovering what people are interested in learning about and what they are willing to pay for the information.

Creating engaging content that will keep your students interested and motivated is also essential. That means using various media, including videos, slides, audio recordings, and interactive elements.

Marketing is also crucial to the success of your online course or workshop. You can promote your lessons in several ways, including through social media, email marketing, and ads on platforms like Facebook and Google. You can also reach out to influencers and websites in your niche to see if they would be interested in promoting your course.

In conclusion, creating and selling an online course or workshop can be a great way to share your expertise with a broader audience and generate passive income. Following the tips outlined in this section can increase your chances of success and reach a larger audience with your course or workshop.

Chapter 9: Building a Website and Monetizing it through Advertising

Building a website and monetizing it through advertising might be an excellent strategy to generate passive income and reach a broad audience. This section will overview the process of building and monetizing a website through advertising and offer tips for success.

First, let's talk about the options for advertising on your website. One of the most popular options is Google AdSense, which allows you to display ads on your website and earn a share of the revenue when visitors click on them. Other options include Mediavine and AdThrive, advertising networks that specialize in working with websites in the food, lifestyle, and parenting niches.

Now, let's discuss tips for success when building a website and monetizing it through advertising.

One of the most critical things you should do is pick a niche in which you are passionate and in which there is a market. That will help you create valuable content that your audience will be interested in and will help you build a loyal following.

It's also important to focus on building an audience for your website. That can include using social media to promote your website and engage with your audience and SEO tactics to improve your website's ranking in search results.

Finally, creating valuable content that your audience will want to read, and share is crucial. That means producing high-quality, well-written articles that provide value to your readers. You can also use visuals like images and videos to make your content more engaging and help it stand out.

Creating a website and monetizing it through advertising is an excellent method to generate passive money while reaching a large audience. Following the tips outlined in this section can increase your chances of success and build a website that generates revenue through advertising.

Chapter 10: Building a Website and Monetizing it through Affiliate Marketing

Both individuals and businesses worldwide use affiliate marketing to monetize their websites. In this model, affiliates earn a commission by promoting the products or services of other companies. The affiliate receives a commission whenever a user clicks on an affiliate link and buys something.

Many affiliate programs are available, such as Amazon Associates, CJ Affiliate, and Commission Junction. These programs offer a wide range of products or services that affiliates can promote,

making it easy to find something that aligns with your website's niche and target audience.
To create a website and promote affiliate products, you'll need to choose a niche and build an audience. You can do this through various methods, such as creating valuable content, using social media to promote your website, and building relationships with your visitors.
Once you've established your website and built an audience, you can start searching for profitable and high-margin affiliate products to promote. Research the products or services of various affiliate marketing programs and find those that correlate with your website's specialty and target demographic.

To increase your chances of success with affiliate marketing, select a field in which you are interested and knowledgeable. That will make creating valuable content easier and build relationships with your audience. Additionally, it's essential to build an engaged and loyal audience, as this will help drive more sales and earn more commissions over time.
Finally, it's essential to be consistent and persistent in promoting affiliate products. That may involve regularly creating new content, promoting your website through social media and other channels, and continuously seeking new

opportunities to encourage high-margin products. You may establish a profitable website and monetize it through affiliate marketing with dedication and hard work.

Chapter 11: Building a Website and Monetizing it through Selling Digital Products

An e-book is a digital book that anyone may read on a computer, tablet, or e-reader device. E-books have become increasingly popular in recent years because they are convenient to access and often cheaper than physical books.

There are many different ways to create an e-book. If you are a writer, you can make your e-content books with a word processor and save them as a PDF file. Many tools and software programs, such as Adobe InDesign or Scrivener, are available to help you create and format your e-books.

Once you have created your e-book, you must upload it to your website. There are a few different options for doing this. One option is to use a plugin or extension to sell digital products directly from your website. That will require you to set up a payment gateway and handle the transaction yourself.

Another option is to use a third-party platform to sell your e-book. These platforms, such as Amazon Kindle Direct Publishing or Gumroad, handle the payment process and often offer additional features such as marketing and analytics tools.

When selling your e-book, choosing a niche that you are passionate about and have expertise in is essential. That will assist you in producing a high-quality product and establishing yourself as an expert in your sector. Building an audience is also crucial for success. You can do this through social media marketing, guest blogging, and email marketing.

In addition to creating a great product and building an audience, it is also essential to focus on delivering excellent customer service. Responding to inquiries and issues promptly and professionally can help build trust with your customers and encourage repeat business.

Chapter 12: Building a Website and Monetizing it through Selling Physical Products

Physical products, tangible goods, have a physical presence and can be touched, held, and used. These can be anything from clothing and accessories to home goods, electronics, and even food and beverages. Selling physical products online has become increasingly popular in recent years, thanks to the convenience and reach of the internet.

There are several ways to sell physical products online, including setting up your e-commerce website, using an online marketplace such as Amazon or Etsy, or even using social media platforms to sell directly to customers. Each choice has advantages and disadvantages, so carefully examine which is best for you and your company.

When setting up your e-commerce website, you have complete control over your site's design, branding, and functionality. That can be a great option if you have a unique product or want to build a strong brand identity. However, it might be more time-consuming and resource-intensive to establish and maintain. You will also be responsible for driving traffic to your site, which can be challenging if you are starting.

Using an online marketplace can be an easier and more cost-effective way to get started, as these platforms already have a large customer base and handle many technical details for you. However, you will typically have to pay a fee for each sale, and you may need more control over the look and feel of your product listings.

Social media platforms can also be an excellent way to sell physical products, particularly if you already have a large following on a particular platform. You can use your profile or create a business page to showcase your products and use the platform's built-in tools to process orders and payments. However, it can be harder to scale your business using this approach, and you may have to pay for advertising to reach a wider audience.

Regardless of your choice, there are a few key things to remember when selling physical products online. First, it's essential to have high-quality photos and detailed product descriptions to give customers a good sense of what they are buying. You should also have a straightforward returns policy and be prepared to handle customer inquiries and complaints professionally and promptly. Finally, consider offering discounts or promotions to encourage customer loyalty and drive sales.

With careful planning and attention to detail, selling physical products online can be rewarding and successful. By understanding your options and choosing the right approach for your business, you can build a solid online presence and reach a wider audience than you ever could with a traditional brick-and-mortar store.

Sourcing products

Identifying suppliers and wholesalers is an essential step in selling physical products online. A supplier is a company that provides the raw materials or finished products that you will sell. At the same time, a wholesaler is a company that buys products in bulk from suppliers and resells them to retailers (like you) at a higher price.

There are several ways to find suppliers and wholesalers for your online business. One option is to attend trade shows and industry events to meet with potential partners and learn about their products and pricing. You can also search online directories and databases, such as ThomasNet or Alibaba, which list various suppliers and wholesalers. Finally, you can reach out to manufacturers directly to see if they offer wholesale prices to retailers.

Once you have identified potential suppliers and wholesalers, it's crucial to negotiate prices and terms that work for your business. That can involve discussing minimum order quantities, payment terms, and shipping costs. Before you begin negotiating, it's a good idea to have a clear image of your budget and margins so you know what you can afford and what terms you're ready to accept.

Managing inventory is another important aspect of selling physical products online. That involves keeping track of what products you have in stock, how much of each product you have, and when you need to reorder. It's essential to balance having enough inventory to meet customer demand and not so much that you tie up too much capital in unsold products. Several tools and software programs are available to help you manage your inventory and keep track of sales and reorder points.

In summary, identifying suppliers and wholesalers, negotiating prices and terms, and managing inventory are all crucial considerations when selling physical products online. You can ensure a smooth and profitable operation by carefully planning and executing these aspects of your business.

Setting up the website

One of the first considerations you must make when creating a website to sell physical things is which platform to utilize. Several options are available, including popular e-commerce platforms like Shopify and WooCommerce. Shopify is a turnkey solution that provides everything you need to set up and run an online store, including hosting, payment processing, and various customizable templates and design options. It's easy to use and has a wide range of features, making it a good choice for many small businesses. However, it does come with a monthly fee and transaction fees for each sale.

WooCommerce is an open-source e-commerce plugin for WordPress, a popular content management system (CMS). This option gives you more flexibility in design and customization, but it requires some technical know-how to set up and maintain. It's a good option for those who are comfortable with WordPress and want more control over their site.

Once you have chosen a platform, the next step is to design and set up your website. That involves selecting a layout, colour scheme, and overall look and feel that reflects your brand and appeals to your target audience. Creating a user-friendly shopping experience with straightforward navigation, easy-to-use filters, and high-quality product photos is also essential.

Finally, you will need to set up payment and shipping options for your online store. That involves choosing a payment processor (such as PayPal or Stripe) and setting up the necessary accounts and integrations. You will also need to decide how you will handle shipping, including which carriers you will use, what shipping options you will offer (such as the flat rate or calculated based on weight), and whether you will provide free shipping or a fee.

In summary, setting up a website to sell physical products online involves choosing a platform, designing the site, and setting up payment and shipping options. By carefully planning and executing these steps, you can create a professional and user-friendly online store ready to start accepting orders.

Marketing and promotion

Once your website is set up and ready, the next step is marketing and promoting your products to attract customers. One of the first steps will be to identify and target your audience. That involves understanding who your ideal customers are, what they are interested in, and where they are likely to be found online. That might assist you in tailoring your marketing efforts and increasing their efficacy.

The next stage is to create a marketing plan. That can include several strategies, such as social media marketing, email marketing, and PPC marketing. Platforms such as Facebook, Instagram, Instagram and Pinterest may be effective ways to reach out to potential customers, especially if your product is visually appealing. Email marketing enables you to send personalized messages to a subscriber database and could be an effective strategy for developing leads and boosting revenue. Sponsored content, such as Google AdSense or Facebook Ads, is also an efficient method of reaching a broader audience. However, it can be more expensive and requires careful planning and targeting to be effective.

Building an email list is another crucial aspect of marketing and promotion when selling physical products online. That involves collecting email addresses from potential customers and sending them regular newsletters or promotional messages. An email list allows you to build relationships with customers and nurture leads over time, increasing their chances of purchasing. Several tools and software programs are available to help you manage and grow your email list.

In summary, marketing and promotion are crucial to selling physical products online. You can effectively promote your products and drive sales by identifying and targeting your audience, developing a marketing strategy, and building an email list.

Tips for success

One essential tip for success is choosing a niche and identifying your product demand. Although it might be appealing to try to offer a wide range of things, concentrating on a specific location will enable you to stand out and separate yourself from the competitors. It's also essential to do market research to ensure that there is actual demand for the products you are selling. That can involve talking to potential customers, analyzing industry trends, and looking at data from other online stores.

Another important tip is to offer excellent customer service. That can include responding promptly to customer inquiries, offering a hassle-free returns process, and going above and beyond to resolve any issues that may arise. You can build customer loyalty and encourage repeat business by providing a high level of service.

Finally, it's vital to improve and update your product offerings continuously. That can involve introducing new products, revising existing products to make them better, and listening to customer feedback to identify areas for improvement. You can remain ahead of the competition and keep your business thriving by being current and responsive to client requirements.

In summary, success when selling physical products online involves
- choosing a niche and identifying demand,
- offering excellent customer service, and
- continuously improving and updating your product offerings.

Following these tips can build a successful and sustainable online business.

Creating a website and monetizing it through selling real things may be rewarding and profitable. You may build up a professional and user-friendly online store and begin selling your items to a larger audience by following the instructions explained in this e-book.

Identifying and targeting your audience, devising a marketing plan, and providing outstanding customer service is crucial. Selecting a platform and setting up your website to match your brand and provide clients with a seamless buying experience is also critical.

If you're considering selling physical things online, we recommend you jump and get started. You can develop a successful internet business and achieve your entrepreneurial objectives with a little strategy and hard work. Best wishes!

Chapter 13: Start print-on-demand business

Print-on-demand (POD) produces goods only when an order is received instead of making goods in advance and storing them in warehouses. This business model has grown in popularity recently, notably in the e-commerce sector.

Starting a print-on-demand business is a terrific way to start entrepreneurship since it allows you to start small and expand as your firm grows. Starting a print-on-demand business has various advantages, including minimal upfront expenses, flexibility in product offers, and the opportunity to test and iterate on new ideas without incurring substantial risks or expenditures. This e-book will look at the many components of beginning a print-on-demand business and offer advice and solutions.

Research and planning for print-on-demand business

Research and planning for print-on-demand business

Before diving into print-on-demand, initiating research and planning your business is essential. That enables you to make better decisions about your product offerings and company strategy, increasing your chances of success.

One of the first steps in the research and planning process is identifying your target market. To whom do you want to sell your products?

What are their interests and requirements? Understanding your target market will enable you to produce things they will be interested in and efficiently advertise your business to them.

Following that, it is critical to research your competition and its products. Please take a look at what they have to offer.

Setting up your business for print-on-demand business

After you've finished your research and planning, it's time to set up your company for success. Here are some necessary measures to consider:

Choose a platform or provider for print-on-demand: There are several options for print-on-demand services, each with its benefits and costs. Spend time looking into and comparing potential prospects to find the ideal one. Think about the options available, the quality, the turnaround time, and the service.

Design or obtain items to sell: Because your product offerings will be a critical component of your business, it is essential to consider what you will sell. You can design your items using graphic design tools or sourcing products from others.

Establish your web website or digital services: Once your items are ready to sell, you must provide a mechanism for people to buy them. You may do this through your website or third-party service offerings like Etsy or Amazon.

Build your branding and advertising strategy: Consistent brand awareness is essential since your brand represents your company's personality and appearance. Your logo, colour palette, and messaging are examples of this. Create a strategy to advertise your items and reach your target audience. Social media advertising, email campaigns, and content creation are all examples of this.

You can put your business apart from the competition and start making sales in the fascinating world of print-on-demand by complying with these steps and being persistent in your strategies.

Running your business

After starting your print-on-demand firm, you must manage and expand it. Key considerations:

Order processing: Print-on-demand companies must manage order flow and ensure accuracy and efficiency. Maintaining inventory, working with your print-on-demand provider, and informing clients on orders may be needed.

Pricing: Business success depends on product pricing. You must compete while covering costs and making a profit. Check your margins and competitors' manufacturing, shipping, and price.

Service and returns: Customer service drives e-commerce success. Give customers a fair return policy and respond immediately.

Growing and adapting your business: E-commerce is continuously changing. Therefore, you must keep up. That may include adding new products, sales channels, or marketing strategies. Keep track of industry developments and be flexible to grow your firm.

These key areas will help you manage and build your print-on-demand business.

Congratulations for completing the first print-on-demand portion! You should now understand how to launch a business.

To recap, starting a print-on-demand business necessitates the following steps:

Determine your target market as part of your business planning.

- Look into your competition.
- Choose a specialty.
- Prepare a business plan.

Setting up a business:

- Select a print-on-demand platform or service provider, then develop or source items.
- Create an internet store or sales channels.
- Make a brand and marketing plan.

Chapter 14: The Benefits of Starting Small and Scaling up as your Passive Income Streams Grow

Starting small and gradually increasing your passive income sources may be a wise and strategic method to accumulate wealth and financial stability. Here are some of the advantages of this method:

Low risk: Starting small reduces risk and ensures you have the means to weather storms and setbacks. That is especially true if you rely on passive income to sustain yourself and your family.

Starting small also allows you the freedom to pivot and adjust as required. If one passive income stream isn't doing well, you may focus on another without putting too much money into the first.

Building passive income streams can be a learning experience and starting small allows you to make errors and learn from them without endangering your overall financial status.

Scalability: As your passive income streams expand, you can increase your efforts and reinvest your gains in new possibilities. Over time, this can help you compound your wealth and boost your financial stability.

Building numerous modest passive income sources can give a more reliable and varied revenue stream than depending on a large one. That can help safeguard you against market changes and other unforeseeable situations.

Finally, starting small and growing up as your passive income sources increase may be a sensible and strategic strategy for wealth creation and financial stability. You may lay a solid financial foundation by reducing risk, remaining flexible, and generating numerous income streams.

Chapter 15: The Significance of Remaining Motivated and Focused on your Passive Income Objectives

Passive income requires little or no effort to retain and earn. Rental properties, profits from investments, and online enterprises are all examples of passive income streams. While passive income can deliver a consistent source of income without the need for active participation, to successfully establish and sustain a passive income stream, it is critical to be motivated and focused on your passive income objectives.

One of the primary advantages of passive income is that it gives you more time and freedom to accomplish the activities you enjoy. However, keep in mind that creating a passive income stream takes time and work, and it is accessible only to satisfy if you see quick results. To attain your passive income goals, you must stay motivated and focused.

Setting precise, attainable objectives for yourself is one approach to staying motivated. That can keep you on track and give you a sense of accomplishment while you work towards your more meaningful goals. It is also beneficial to surround yourself with positive people who can offer encouragement and advice.

Another key to passive income success is consistency and persistence in your efforts. Building a passive income stream necessitates a long-term mentality as well as the determination to endure in the face of any problems that may arise. Understand that building a passive income stream is a process with hurdles. You must maintain concentration and keep moving forward to attain your passive income goals.

In addition to staying motivated and engaged, you must continually educate yourself on passive income trends and best practices. That helps you identify new opportunities and make informed judgements regarding your passive income techniques.

Overall, staying motivated and focused on your passive income goals is critical for creating and sustaining a solid passive income stream. You may boost your chances of success and reach your passive income goals by creating precise plans, surrounding yourself with encouraging people, being consistent and persistent in your efforts, and constantly educating yourself.

Chapter 16: The Role of a Positive Mindset in Achieving Success with Passive Income Streams

Success with passive income streams requires an optimistic mindset. The term "passive income" refers to a stream of funds that don't necessitate constant effort on your part to keep it going and can provide a reliable income stream with minimal effort. To increase your odds of success with passive income, which have the potential to be a powerful financial instrument, you need to take a proactive and optimistic stance.

Keeping a sunny disposition aid in finding viable solutions. It's easy to quit if you face challenges while trying to establish a passive income source. However, if you take a constructive approach to these challenges, you will be better able to think of innovative solutions and persevere no matter your obstacles.

Keeping an optimistic outlook can aid in accomplishing tasks and achieving success in pursuing passive income. If you're trying to create a passive income stream, it's easy to get discouraged or lose focus. However, keeping an upbeat attitude can help you stay on track and progress.

Positivity is vital for creating a passive income stream, and so is an openness to new prospects. You need to be flexible and willing to try new things if you want to uncover your most excellent passive income strategies. With the right frame of mind, it's much easier to spot promising new avenues and take calculated risks to pursue your passive income targets.

Maintaining an optimistic mindset is key to success with passive income streams. Suppose you approach problems with a solution-oriented mindset, maintain motivation and engagement, and keep an eye out for new opportunities. In that case, you may increase the likelihood of creating a successful and sustainable passive income stream. Keeping a positive outlook on life is beneficial.

Chapter 17: Tips for Maximizing the Potential of Passive Income Streams

A passive income stream generates money for you without you actively doing anything to get it. This type of income is ideal for those who want to supplement this current income or work toward financial independence. However, a systematic approach to passive income is required to realise its potential fully. Consider these suggestions to help you make the most of your passive income opportunities.

Spread out your passive revenue streams to make the most of their potential. Instead of relying on just one source of passive income, you should diversify your holdings. Doing so could make your passive income more secure and less vulnerable to fluctuations.

If you desire a long-term passive income stream, invest in assets with strong growth or constant returns. Real estate investments, dividend-paying equities, and established web enterprises fit this description. Investing in the right assets might boost your passive income streams if you do your research.

Think about the Big picture: If you want to create a passive income stream, you must be willing to invest time and effort over the long haul. Investors can expect market swings and delayed outcomes. Keeping your eye on the long game is the key to overcoming temporary obstacles and realizing the full potential of your passive income streams.

Educate yourself and keep up with the newest developments in your field so you can make educated choices about generating passive income. Reading relevant articles, attending relevant seminars, and consulting appropriate specialists are all viable options. You can maximize your passive income streams and take advantage of new chances if you keep your mind and body active.

To create a passive income stream, you must be consistent and persistent. It's crucial to keep your eye on the prize and keep moving forward, no matter how difficult the going becomes or how many setbacks you experience. You may improve your chances of success and unlock the full potential of your passive income streams by being consistent and persistent in your efforts.

Benefit from Modern Tools: It's simpler than ever to establish and maintain passive income streams. Automation technologies that speed up processes and internet platforms that connect you with new clients or tenants can improve passive income.

Keep your money to make the most of your passive income streams. It would help if you kept your finances in order. Developing a financial plan, saving for the future, and investing in assets that can increase your

Conclusion

You have taken the initial step toward financial independence now that you understand how to generate passive income without spending money. Using the information in this book, you can start earning money while sleeping.

The time and effort you invest initially to establish a passive income stream will pay off handsomely in the long run. A passive income gives you greater control over your life and finances because it provides a constant stream of money that requires little effort.

Avoid rushing through tasks. Instead, devote the necessary time today to establishing multiple passive income streams. You can generate passive income by trading on the stock market, creating digital products, or working with businesses.

To be successful with passive income, you must stay motivated and on track, adhere to your plan, and monitor the market, industry trends, and best business practices. If you stick to these guidelines, you will increase your chances of success and establish the foundation for long-term financial stability.

Explore your alternatives by going out. If you wish to generate income without exerting effort, the world is your oyster.

Hey Dear,

Thank you for purchasing this "How to Make Passive Income with Zero Money".

This book will help you understand passive income with zero money, and I assure you this e-book will help you more than you think.

As an Author-it will help me to understand your reader's need if you leave a review for this book where you purchased it.

Thank you again,

Shakh Sabber Ahmed